This is the story of

$$\left[\ \text{PHOTO}\ \right]$$

My Parents

My parents are _____

and _____

A few things to know about my mother _____

_____

_____

_____

A few things to know about my father _____

_____

_____

_____

How my parents met _____

_____

_____

_____

_____

_____

My Family

Some things to know about my family _____

_____

_____

[PHOTOS & MEMENTOS]

But as for me and my household, we will serve the Lord. JOSHUA 24:15

PHOTOS & MEMENTOS

Before I Was Born

My family prepared for me by ....

....

....

....

....

My parents' prayers for me ....

....

....

Prayers from my family and church ....

....

....

Children are a gift from the Lord. PSALMS 127:3

The Miracle of My Arrival

My name ....

Its meaning ....

My birthplace ....

Memories of our first moments together ....

....

....

....

....

BIRTH DATE	TIME	LENGTH	WEIGHT

MY HANDPRINT(S)

MY FOOTPRINT(S)

PHOTOS & MEMENTOS

On That Special Day

The most popular song _____

Our nation's leader _____

The cost of a cup of coffee _____

The top news headlines _____

_____

_____

Other special things about this day _____

_____

_____

_____

_____

My Dedication / Baptism

Date _____

Location _____

People who attended _____

_____

_____

_____

Prayer _____

_____

_____

_____

_____

PHOTOS & MEMENTOS

My Spiritual Family

The people who support my spiritual growth are _____

_____

_____

_____

A few things to know about them _____

_____

_____

_____

Their prayers for me _____

_____

_____

_____

This little

light of mine

I'm going to

let it shine

MONTHLY MILESTONES

[PHOTOS & MEMENTOS]

MONTH

I love _____

_____

_____

_____

I don't like _____

_____

_____

_____

I learned _____

_____

_____

_____

_____

An unforgettable memory _____

_____

_____

_____

_____

This month's prayer for me _____

_____

Two

I love _____

_____

_____

I don't like _____

_____

_____

I learned _____

_____

_____

_____

An unforgettable memory _____

_____

_____

_____

This month's prayer for me _____

_____

[PHOTOS & MEMENTOS]

[PHOTOS & MEMENTOS]

MONTH

Three

I love _____

_____

_____

I don't like _____

_____

_____

I learned _____

_____

_____

_____

An unforgettable memory _____

_____

_____

_____

This month's prayer for me _____

_____

Four

I love ....

....

....

....

I don't like ....

....

....

....

I learned ....

....

....

....

....

An unforgettable memory ....

....

....

....

....

This month's prayer for me ....

....

[PHOTOS & MEMENTOS]

[PHOTOS & MEMENTOS]

Five

I love _____

_____

_____

_____

I don't like _____

_____

_____

_____

I learned _____

_____

_____

_____

An unforgettable memory _____

_____

_____

_____

This month's prayer for me _____

_____

MONTH

I love ....

....

....

....

I don't like ....

....

....

....

I learned ....

....

....

....

....

An unforgettable memory ....

....

....

....

This month's prayer for me ....

....

[PHOTOS & MEMENTOS]

[PHOTOS & MEMENTOS]

Seven

I love _____

_____

_____

_____

I don't like _____

_____

_____

_____

I learned _____

_____

_____

_____

_____

An unforgettable memory _____

_____

_____

_____

_____

This month's prayer for me _____

_____

Eight

I love ....

....

....

....

I don't like ....

....

....

....

I learned ....

....

....

....

An unforgettable memory ....

....

....

....

This month's prayer for me ....

....

[PHOTOS & MEMENTOS]

Nine

I love ....

....

....

....

I don't like ....

....

....

....

I learned ....

....

....

....

....

An unforgettable memory ....

....

....

....

....

This month's prayer for me ....

....

Ten

I love _____

_____

_____

_____

I don't like _____

_____

_____

_____

I learned _____

_____

_____

_____

An unforgettable memory _____

_____

_____

_____

This month's prayer for me _____

_____

PHOTOS & MEMENTOS

[PHOTOS & MEMENTOS]

Eleven

I love _____

_____

_____

_____

I don't like _____

_____

_____

_____

I learned _____

_____

_____

_____

_____

An unforgettable memory _____

_____

_____

_____

_____

This month's prayer for me _____

_____

Twelve

I love _____

I don't like _____

_____

_____

_____

_____

_____

_____

I learned _____

An unforgettable memory _____

_____

_____

_____

_____

_____

_____

_____

_____

This month's prayer for me _____

_____

PHOTOS & MEMENTOS

You are **beautiful,** *my darling,* beautiful beyond words.

SONG OF SOLOMON 4:1

A FIRST TIME
FOR
EVERYTHING

Meaningful Moments

My First Bath

My First Outing

My First Smile

My First Laugh

[PHOTOS & MEMENTOS]

*Our mouths were filled with laughter,
our tongues with songs of joy.* PSALMS 126:2-3

My First Tooth

_____

_____

My First Solid Food

_____

_____

My First Time Sitting Up

My First Time Crawling

$$\begin{bmatrix} \text{PHOTOS \& MEMENTOS} \end{bmatrix}$$

My First Time Standing

My First Steps

_____

_____

$$\Big[\text{PHOTOS \& MEMENTOS} \Big]$$

*He set my feet on a rock and gave me
a firm place to stand.* PSALMS 40:2

My First Word

My First Haircut

My First _____

_____

_____

[PHOTOS & MEMENTOS]

My First _____

_____

_____

My First Holidays

My First New Year's

My First Valentine's Day

Love is patient, love is kind. 1 CORINTHIANS 13:4

My First Easter

[PHOTOS & MEMENTOS]

He is not here; he has risen! LUKE 24:6

My First Mother's Day

_____

_____

[PHOTOS & MEMENTOS]

My First Father's Day

My First Independence Day

My First Thanksgiving

My First Christmas

[PHOTOS & MEMENTOS]

I bring you good news that will bring great joy to all people. LUKE 2:10

My First _____

_____

_____

My First _____

_____

_____

[PHOTOS & MEMENTOS]

My First Birthday

How we celebrated _____

_____

_____

People who celebrated with me _____

_____

_____

A few of my favorite things

SONG _____

FOOD _____

BOOK _____

TOY _____

ACTIVITIES _____

May he grant you your heart's desire and fulfill all your plans! PSALMS 20:4

[PHOTOS & MEMENTOS]

[PHOTOS & MEMENTOS]

ISBN: 9780593690536

ART © NADIA GRAPES/SHUTTERSTOCK.COM
BOOK DESIGN BY KATY BROWN
EDITED BY CLARA SONG LEE

PRINTED IN CHINA
1 3 5 7 9 10 8 6 4 2

[PHOTOS & MEMENTOS]